The Bayeux Tapestry

THE STORY OF THE MOST FAMOUS OF MEDIEVAL EMBROIDERIES

CONTENTS

OREP
EDITIONS

INTRODUCTION

The Bayeux Tapestry is one of the most represented works of art across the globe. Even before discovering it within the museum where it is displayed, each and every one of us has seen at least one illustration of one of the 58 scenes it comprises. Be it from our childhood days, in a history book on the Middle Ages, or simply reproduced on one of the many luxury products or everyday items that are distributed throughout the world (cushions, porcelain, jewellery, clothing, umbrellas and gadgets of all sorts).

And it always comes as a surprise to the visitor who never imagined it to be as long, or as narrow, or as lively or as colourful as it is in real life. It is a source of enthralment for all visitors, from the curious tourist, to the historian, via the young child fascinated by the animals that adorn its borders, or the artist impressed by the inventiveness of its scenography, not forgetting the embroidery enthusiast. No-one is insensitive to this story, dating back around 950 years, which is told in the form of image and Latin text.

DESCRIPTION OF THE TAPESTRY

Of a height of 48 to 51 centimetres, the Tapestry – for we have become accustomed to naming it so – measures 68.38 metres in length. It comprises nine sections which are attached to each other by means of seams that are more or less difficult to distinguish, hence the number of sections having for a long time been underestimated. In varying lengths, the longest measures 13.90 metres and the smallest, 2.43 metres.

The Tapestry is divided into three zones. The central zone – the most important – is around 33 centimetres high and, over 58 scenes, tells the story of the whys and wherefores of William of Normandy's conquest of England. The central part of the Tapestry is framed by two borders, each of approximately 7 centimetres in height, decorated essentially with familiar or fantasy animals, of fables by Phaedrus, inspired by Aesop, or of scenes of work in the fields.

The Tapestry's uniqueness lies in the fact that it is the only narrative church hanging that has survived, almost intact, to the present day. Over and above its missing final metres - if indeed it was ever completed – the work has also suffered a number of accidents: 681 holes and tears in the central band, 23 damaged linen yarns, over 400 reinforcements added and stains, most likely caused by wax from nearby candles. Its restoration during the third quarter of the 19th century is evident due to the vivid colours of certain chemically dyed woollen features on the front side and to fragments sewn onto the canvas on the back side. Despite its great fragility, the work has survived nine and a half centuries and continues to be admired every year by around 500,000 visitors.

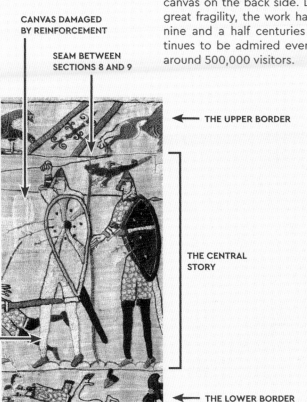

CANVAS DAMAGED
BY REINFORCEMENT

SEAM BETWEEN
SECTIONS 8 AND 9

← THE UPPER BORDER

THE CENTRAL
STORY

RESTORATION →

← THE LOWER BORDER

Scene 1. King Edward and Harold.

1066 AND THE YEAR OF THE THREE KINGS OF ENGLAND

Let's take the time to introduce you to the main characters of its story.

The Tapestry opens with a depiction of **King Edward**, known to posterity as Edward the Confessor, because of his great piousness. He was even known as a saint after he was canonised in 1161.

He was born circa 1005 in Islip in Oxfordshire, from the marriage between the King of England Æthelred II the Unready and Emma, the daughter of Richard I, Duke of Normandy. Driven out of England by a Danish invasion, he took refuge within the Normandy court for around 30 years, a period during which the English throne passed from his mother's husband, the Danish King Cnut (†1035), to the latter's two sons, Harold Harefoot (†1040) and Harthacanute (†1042), Edward's step-brother. He only recovered the throne of England in 1042, to be crowned in 1043. A few years later, having no direct heir, he designated Duke William of Normandy as his successor, his marriage with Godwin's daughter, Edith, apparently never having been consummated. He died on the 5th of January 1066 and his death led to a war of succession.

Edward appears four times throughout the Tapestry. In scene 1, easily recognisable thanks to his fleur-de-lis crown, he welcomes two other characters to his palace. We then discover him once more listening to his brother-in-law Harold (scene 25). Finally, we can watch his last agony (scene 27) and are twice presented with his dead body (scenes 26 and 28).

Harold Godwinson is also present in the Tapestry's opening scene. His name is mentioned a total of 16 times throughout the story, and he is also depicted in several other scenes, without being mentioned in the Latin text that runs throughout the embroidery.

Born circa 1022, Harold was the son of Godwin, the Earl of Wessex and of Gytha Thorkelsdóttir, the sister of a Danish *jarl* (equivalent to an earl) and hence related to the Danish King Cnut. He was one of a large sibship. Edith, his sister, was King Edward's wife. One of his brothers, Tostig, was to influence the turn of events during the autumn of 1066, whilst two other brothers, Leofwine and Gyrth, supported him in his battle against the Norman invader. Harold inherited from his father in 1053, to become the most powerful nobleman in the Kingdom of England after the king. Acknowledged as the Duke of the English (*Dux Anglorum* in the Tapestry), he claimed the crown, which he obtained on the 6th of January 1066. His reign was to be short-lived. He was killed on the 14th of October 1066 at the Battle of Hastings.

William of Normandy is depicted for the first time in scene 12 of the Bayeux Tapestry. He is represented on several occasions, by fifteen mentions of his name and by his obvious depiction, without caption. He is, nevertheless, a little less present on the canvas than Harold. William was born circa 1027 in Falaise, from the union between the Duke of Normandy, Robert the Magnificent and Herleva (also known as Arlette), the daughter of a local craftsman, thought to have

Scene 12.
Duke William of Normandy.

been a tanner. He became the 7th Duke of Normandy in 1035, upon his father's death, but struggled to assert his position due to his illegitimacy and his very young age. His victory at the Battle of Val ès Dunes (1047) sealed his authority over the Norman barons and the Battles of Mortemer (1054) and Varaville (1058) put a permanent end to the King of France, Henri I's claims to the Duchy. Around the year 1050, William married Matilda, the daughter of Baldwin V, Count of Flanders and of Adela of France, sister to the French King Henri I.

As the first cousin once removed of King Edward, William was not the only pretender to the English throne in 1066. Yet his lineage and the promise the dying king had made to him rendered his claim perfectly legitimate. Meanwhile, Harald Hardrada, the King of Norway, also claimed the throne, based on a pact between the King Harthacanute and the Scandinavian King Magnus to whom Harald had succeeded. William left him enough time to land in Yorkshire, in the northeast of England, and to challenge the English army at Stamford Bridge, where he was killed on the 25th of September 1066. The Norman army then crossed the English Channel and set up camp in the south-east of England, Harold had no choice but to advance and confront them at the Battle of Hastings on the 14th of October 1066. Harold's death and the Norman victory over the annihilated English army was the first step in William's journey to London, via Dover, Canterbury, Southwark, Wallingford and Berkhamsted. The Norman duke was crowned King of England in Westminster Abbey on Christmas Day 1066.

HISTORY TOLD
BY THE BAYEUX TAPESTRY

The story begins in 1064 (scene 1). Edward, King of England for the past 22 years, married to Edith, the daughter of Godwin of Wessex - the second most important person in the kingdom - has no direct heir. In 1053, he already designated William the Bastard, Duke of Normandy, as his successor. He entrusts his brother-in-law Harold with the mission of travelling to Normandy to confirm to Duke William that he is the future King of England. The scene takes place in a royal residence, most probably Winchester Palace.

HAROLD GODWINSON'S JOURNEY

Harold leads a small troop of horsemen and heads to southeast England (scene 2). The depiction of their ride is somewhat reminiscent of a hunting party - Harold, holding a falcon on his wrist, is preceded by a group of hounds.

Scene 2. Harold.

After riding past the tree adorned with splendid interlacing which marks the end of the scene, Harold and his companions stop at Bosham, a harbour town near Chichester, from where it is easy to embark for a Channel crossing. The Romanesque church (fig. 5) and Harold's lordly manor are both represented (scene 3).

After recuperating, by praying, eating and drinking, the time comes for Harold and his companions to board. The men cross the foreshore bare-legged, loading the falcon and dogs onto their vessels (scene 4), built according to Viking tradition.

Scene 3.
The church
at Bosham.

Their flat base means they can be dragged up onto the shore. They are equipped with oars that are useful for warping and approaching manoeuvres, along with a rudder to steer them in the high seas and a large sail that thrusts them forward when filled with wind (scenes 4 to 6). This is highlighted in the Latin text, 'And with the sails swelled with the wind, he came to the land belonging to the Count Guy' (scene 5). As the wind turns to storm, Harold's boats are driven towards the Ponthieu coast, to the north of Normandy.

Scenes 5–6–7. Harold taken prisoner by Guy of Ponthieu.

HAROLD'S CAPTIVITY

Barely do they set foot on French soil, when the English are taken prisoner by a troop commanded by Guy I of Ponthieu, the lord of these lands and one of the Duke of Normandy's vassals (scene 7). They are taken to the castle of Beaurain, in the Canche valley (scene 8). In a hall, as suggested by the arches supported by columns, Guy, seated on a throne, sets his conditions for Harold's release, most probably in the form of the payment of a ransom. Their conversation is overheard by a character, partly concealed by a pillar (scene 9). Could he be the one who will later inform William of Normandy of Harold's captivity?

Scene 9.
In the castle
at Beaurain.

Whatever the case, William's messengers are welcomed by Guy of Ponthieu, recognisable thanks to his sumptuous costume and his axe, a symbol of his command. Only one character is named - a dwarf by the name of Turold, the significance of whom remains a mystery to us (scene 10). Upon their return to Normandy, the messengers report on their mission to Duke William (scenes 11-12). They are accompanied by an English emissary, recognisable thanks to his long hair and moustache – highly distinctive signs, for the French characters are never moustached and have their necks shaved (scene 12). Negotiations lead to Guy personally accompanying Harold, to hand him over to William (scene 13). This encounter most likely takes place in Eu, located at the northern extremity of Normandy.

Scene 13. Harold and Guy of Ponthieu face William.

HAROLD'S TRIP TO NORMANDY

William invites Harold to stay in Normandy. An initial encounter takes place in a sumptuous residence that can only be the ducal palace in Rouen (scene 14). Before William, who carefully listens to his story, Harold gestures and tells of the reason for his travels to Normandy.

The following scene appears to be a digression (scene 15). A priest, recognisable by his tonsure, has his hand placed on the cheek of a woman named Ælfgyva, whilst, in the lower border, a man can be seen exhibiting himself. It is tempting to interpret this episode as a reference to a scandalous incident, yet certain historians believe it to represent the engagement of one of William's daughters to Harold.

WOMEN IN THE TAPESTRY

Of the 626 characters depicted on the Tapestry, only six are women: three in the central band and three in the borders.

The first to appear is named Ælfgyva (scene 15). Although her name means nothing to the present-day spectator, we can suppose that it was known to her contemporaries via a scandalous event. For do we not see her receiving absolution from a priest, whilst, in the lower border, a man is exhibiting his genitals?

Although unnamed in the Latin text, the second woman can be no other than Queen Edith (scene 27). She is seen seated at the foot of King Edward, her dying husband's bed, during his last instants. Her face is partly concealed by her veil, suggesting that she is weeping.

The third woman is anonymous (scene 47). She is holding the hand of a young child as they leave a house near Hastings which the soldiers have set on fire. These two characters symbolise the widow and the orphan.

All three are wearing loose-fitting clothes that cover their bodies to the ground. Their heads are veiled.

The three other women appear, naked, in the lower border (scene 13) and in the upper border (scene 48). If we relate these women to the images in the central band, we note that they appear when the battle is about to be engaged. Are we to consider them as victims of rape? Their attitude is all the more difficult to interpret for this scene of the embroidery has been restored.

9

S:VE NERVNT:ADMONTE MICHAELIS

Scenes 16–17. The Mont Saint-Michel Bay.

WILLIAM'S MILITARY EXPEDITION IN BRITTANY

The narration now focuses on an army manoeuvring in the Mont Saint-Michel bay, where we can see the abbey poised on its rock, protruding onto the upper border (scene 16).

William is seen on horseback wearing ring armour covered with triangular leather patches and holding a « *bâton de commandement* [1] » in his right hand. Several Norman horsemen fall victim to the sinking sand (scene 17), from which Harold bravely frees them. As soon as they arrive in Brittany, the Normans engage in battle before Dol, the lord of which – Rivallon - has called upon William to help him in his revolt against his suzerain, Conan II of Rennes, Duke of Brittany. The latter manages to escape from the fortress by means of a rope (scene 18).

Scene 18. Dol Castle.

He retreats to Rennes, the capital of his duchy, with the Normans in pursuit (scene 18). He finally finds refuge in Dinan, where he admits defeat (scene 19). He hands over the town keys to William at the end of a spear (scene 20). After this expedition in Brittany, William honours Harold by dubbing him. He arms him with a coat of mail, a helmet and a sword (scene 21). In doing so, he makes Harold his obligee.

1. rod of command.

:TRANSIERVNT :FLVMEN: COSNONIS: ET VENERV

hIC: hAROLD:DVX: TRAhEBAT:EOS :·

DEARENA

HAROLD'S OATH

William returns to Normandy and heads for the castle in Bayeux (scene 22), then most probably to Bayeux Cathedral, despite it not being specifically named (scene 23). In the absence of any text to enlighten us, we can only imagine the nature of his oath. The most credible theory is that Harold is committing himself to acknowledge William as King Edward's successor, the day the latter comes to pass. In keeping with the conventions of the time, such an oath is considered sacred and can in no way be broken without being condemned by God for lying under oath. Harold's supporters will later claim that this oath was extorted through cunning.

The first pages of the history of the Norman Conquest of England end here.

Scene 23. Harold's oath.

VENIT:AD:EDVVARD: REGE M:~ h

Scene 25. Edward receiving Harold.

HAROLD'S RETURN TO ENGLAND

His mission accomplished, Harold boards and heads for England, where his arrival does not go unnoticed (scene 24). A look-out and four faces can be seen at the windows of a building overlooking the beach, as they peer at his berthing boat. Harold and his squire hurry to their horses to meet as soon as possible with King Edward.

Edward welcomes them to what could well be Westminster Palace in London (scene 25). With tired face and stooped body, the 60 year-old king is approaching his death. He listens to Harold, who seems to be ill at ease as he relates the events he has just experienced to the king.

With no further transition, we then view Edward's funeral on the 5th of January 1066, in St. Peter's Abbey (Westminster), which he has had built (scene 26). The labourer fixing a cockerel to the belfry suggests its fresh completion. The hand of God blessing the building also indicates its recent consecration, on the 28th of December 1065. The king's body is carried by eight men, in the company of a group of priests singing hymns, and two children sounding small bells. Curiously, the king's last instants are only depicted after his burial (scenes 27-28). With support from a servant, he is blessed by a priest who has not taken the time to shave, a seated woman at the foot of his bed is weeping into her veil. Edward is talking to a lavishly dressed man. Their hand gestures suggest that a promise has been made. From the Anglo-Saxon Chronicle, we learn that Harold and his sister, Queen Edith, are present during the king's last instants, during which he entrusts the Queen and the throne of England to Harold.

Scene 26. King Edward's funeral procession heads for Westminster Abbey.

It is precisely upon this claim that Harold's supporters declare that he is not guilty of breaking his oath by taking the English throne, for Edward changed his mind on his death bed, naming Harold as his successor. The lower part of this scene depicts Edward being placed in a shroud in the presence of a priest.

Scenes 27–28. Edward's death.

Scenes 29–30. Harold takes the throne.

HAROLD'S CORONATION

The day after Edward's death, the *Witenagemot*, an assembly comprised of earls, lords, members of the senior clergy, endorse the choice of Harold as the new King of England (scene 29). Represented seated on a raised throne, he is wearing a fleur-de-lis crown and holding a sceptre in his right hand, and an orb and cross in his left hand, both signs of royalty. A naked sword, symbol of temporal power, is handed to him.

The ceremony is blessed by Stigand, the Archbishop of Canterbury (scene 30) and legitimised by the applauding crowd (scene 31).

With no chronological link between events - we pass from January to April-May 1066 - when a worried crowd points to a star which, in fact, was Halley's Comet (scene 32). This ball of fire with a hair-like tail feeds superstition. In the following scene (scene 33), even Harold seems alarmed. The lower border depicts a phantom fleet, in anticipation of the Norman invasion fleet.

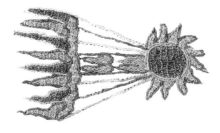

Scene 32.

WILLIAM'S PREPARATIONS TO CONQUER ENGLAND

Once more, the narrator leaves us to freely interpret. We know that an English boat lands in Normandy (scene 34). We suppose that a messenger has come to report on the situation in England. The encounter takes place in a Norman castle, in the presence of William's half-brother, Odo of Conteville, the Bishop of Bayeux. William orders for a fleet to be built. The presence of a labourer, probably a master carpenter, holding a broad axe – a tool used to plane wood – suggests the immediacy of the execution of this order (scene 35).

Scene 35.

Lumberjacks fell trees, carpenters chop planks and shipwrights build ships which, once complete, are dragged to the sea and attached to a berthing pole (scene 36). The Tapestry informs us neither of the name of the naval construction yards, nor the site where the fleet is gathered, such information coming from written sources. The site is the estuary of the Dives, a small coastal river located in the present-day *département* of Calvados. We are also ignorant as to the movement of these boats between Dives and Saint-Valéry-sur-Somme, from where the fleet sets off for England. We are only invited to observe them being loaded with coats of mail, swords, javelins, nasal helmets and victuals in the form of wine vats, transported by cart, drawn by men (scene 37).

Scene 36. Building the boats.

IVH ETVENIT AD PEVENE

Scene 38. The Norman fleet.

THE CROSSING

On the 27th of September 1066, by south winds and ebbing tide, before sunset, William leads a group of horsemen to board several ships (scene 38). Exactly how many vessels cross the English Channel? Sources contradict. The figure of 696 put forward by the poet, Wace, seems more plausible than the 3,000 ships claimed by the chronicler Baldric of Dol. Whereas certain ships are new and have been donated by William's brothers and barons, others belonging to the ducal fleet are requisitioned from fishermen in the Norman ports. William's genius lies in the fact that he has an army of horsemen, accompanied by their mounts, travel along with his infantrymen. Placed alongside the planking, they are to endure a crossing that will take the entire night. At dawn, the *Mora*, the flagship offered by Matilda to her husband and recognisable thanks to a standard adorned with a cross, will need to heave-to near the English coast pending the arrival of the smaller, slower and more heavily laden vessels.

COLOURS

The greyish white of the linen canvas that serves as the base of the work is one of the Tapestry's predominant colours, even if it fails to particularly draw our attention. Our gaze focuses more readily on the embroidery, produced using woollen yarn coloured using natural dyes applied directly to the fleece.

Three colorants offer a relatively large range of colours. Reds are obtained using madder. Yellows are obtained using weld, and blues from woad. Greens are the result of a blend of weld and woad, but can also come from altered colours that were originally blue.

The yarn used to restore the Tapestry in the 19th century is chemically dyed. Its sometimes excessively vivid colours contrast with the gentle tones of the 11th century embroidery, making it easy to recognise.

Scene 39. The horses leave their boats.

THE LANDING

The fleet lands in Pevensey, on the southeast coast of England (scene 39). William's choice of this former Roman port, located alongside a lagoon, is in no way fortuitous. He knows that the road is clear. Harold has sent a fleet to London for the winter and has granted leave to the *fyrd*, a contingent of civilian recruits. Furthermore, he is to face a Norwegian invasion in the north, led by King Harald Hardrada and supported by one of Harold's brothers, Tostig. The horses effortlessly leave their vessels and, once unloaded, the latter are dragged onto the shore and their masts unstepped. The first horsemen set off towards Hastings, located around 12 miles to the east of Pevensey.

LIFE IN THE CAMP

Although food has been loaded onto the ships, further victuals need to be found to feed an army estimated at seven to eight thousand men. Resorting to pillaging is also an excellent way of depriving the enemy of food supplies.

Scenes 40 to 43. Pillaging and mealtime.

Armed horsemen, in the company of civilians, scour the English countryside looking for livestock. Modest houses, with one single door, can be seen in the background of these scenes of plunder. A butcher prepares to kill a sheep as a bullock tries to escape and a pig has already been caught (scene 40).

The Latin text unusually provides the name of one of the horsemen – Wadard – suggesting that his role in this operation is deemed to be important. Could he be the intendant? (scene 41)

Our attention is now drawn to the preparation of a meal. Pieces of meat on skewers are ready for cooking, whereas a cauldron hanging from a bar placed on forked sticks is licked by the flames. A cook uses tongs to remove food from the stove (scene 42). Servants pass chickens on skewers to soldiers who eat on their overturned shields placed on trestles. One man blows a horn to announce that the meal is ready. A table of honour in the form of a horseshoe is set and presided over by the Bishop Odo, who blesses the meal comprised of fish and a beverage which is most likely wine (scene 43).

Scene 44. Odo of Conteville, William of Normandy and Robert of Mortain.

Once the meal is over, William meets with his two half-brothers, Odo, the Bishop of Bayeux, and Robert, Count of Mortain, in a built edifice with a triangular roof. This scene (scene 44) contrasts with the previous outdoor scenes. They decide to build a fortification in Hastings. Two labourers appear to be quarrelling with spades, whereas other workers are busy building a mound, an earthen knoll to be used as the base of the future wooden castle (scene 45).

A messenger brings news to William of Harold's victory over the Norwegian troops (scene 46). The King Harald Hardrada and his ally, Tostig Godwinson, have both been killed at Stamford Bridge, to the east of York, during the battle that took place there on the 25th of September. In forced marches, Harold heads to the south of England, where he intends to confront William with a reorganised army.

THE BATTLE OF HASTINGS

William takes advantage of the time left before Harold's army arrives to best prepare the terrain. Orders are given to destroy anything likely to hinder troop movements. Hence, a vast manor from which a woman and child flee, is burnt (scene 47). The Tapestry remains silent on any failed negotiations between the two camps that render the battle inevitable.

William leaves the town of Hastings at dawn on the 14th of October 1066. His body is protected by a coat of mail; his head is covered with a hood of mail, upon which a helmet is placed; his legs are covered with mail gaiters and he is carrying a sword on his side. He is given a stallion and leads his troops (scene 48). Here, the accent is placed on the cavalry, whose power, mobility and striking capacity are what will make the difference during combat.

Scene 48. William.

Scene 51. The Norman forces.

The horsemen gradually accelerate their pace and are preceded by standard bearers, in turn preceded by Odo, the warrior bishop, who, in abidance with the interdiction for men of the church to spill blood, is carrying a three-headed club which he will use during combat, and by William, on a pale-coated horse, carrying a « *bâton de commandement* » (scenes 48-49).

The scouts of both armies keep watch on their respective enemies. William questions Vital on Harold's approaching troops (scene 49), whilst Harold, beside a harmonious group of trees at the top of Senlac Hill, which is elegantly depicted in stem stitch, questions the sentry who is running towards him (scene 50).

After this long prologue, William harangues his troops, inviting them to engage in combat with courage and wisdom. On the Tapestry, these horsemen occupy almost the entire scene. The foot soldiers in front of them are ignored, the Tapestry then focusing on the archers advancing on foot (scene 51).

Scene 50. Harold and a sentry.

Scene 51. The confrontation.

Historical texts inform us that the Normans, in the centre, are led by William, assisted by Bishop Odo and Robert of Mortain. The left flank, led by Alan of Brittany, is formed of Breton soldiers. The right flank, comprised of Flemish and French soldiers, is commanded by Robert de Beaumont. All three lines are deployed across a width of around 800 - 1,000m (875 - 1,100 yards).

The Normans launch the attack at around 9am. They find themselves face to face with a wall of English shields. In the centre of his army, Harold has placed the *thegns*, members of the aristocracy, and the *housecarls*, elite troops of Danish origin. He has armed his flanks with the *fyrd*, a contingent of commoners, who are poorly equipped and with little training in handling weapons. The bodies of the dead, struck by arrows, occupy the lower border (scene 51).

Although the designers of the Tapestry have chosen to simplify representations of both camps - the horsemen are Norman and the foot soldiers English – their narration offers explicit details of this battle that is to leave a mark on their contemporaries.

Here, they depict the death of Leofwine and Gyrth, two of Harold's still loyal brothers, even if Gyrth had nevertheless tried to dissuade Harold from giving battle. He was afraid of the divine punishment that would inevitably fall upon his brother for breaking the oath he made on holy relics. After this episode, action intensifies. The heavy axes held in both hands by the English, wreak havoc throughout the French ranks. One horse receives a fatal blow to the head (scene 52).

WEAPONS

Defensive weapons included conical nasal helmets which were worn on a hood of mail, coats of mail which covered the body to knee level, shields that were generally almond-shaped – and more rarely round – and which were attached to the arm by means of straps. A larger range of offensive weapons was used. The horsemen's spears, which measured at least two metres in length, although very heavy, were generally used as javelins, which were thrown at their adversaries. They were also used during frontal collisions, when secured under the arm.

A gonfalon, a standard with three flames at its extremity, was sometimes attached to a pole. The sword was used for close combat. It was brandished in one hand, whereas both hands were used to hold the axe. The latter was only used by the English.

The archers carried large bows with which they fired barbed arrows, taken directly from their quivers, which were attached next to their right hand. The mace was the only blunt weapon used. These stones with trilobate carved heads where placed on a wooden handle.

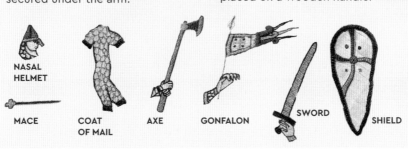

NASAL HELMET

MACE   COAT OF MAIL   AXE   GONFALON   SWORD   SHIELD

The Latin phrase pays homage to combatants from both camps, 'Here the English and the French fell together in combat.' The English are grouped together on a hill from where they overlook a ditch spiked with poles upon which the Norman horses become impaled. Those who manage to pass the obstacle are stopped in their tracks. A blue horse breaks its neck. The head of a mustard-coloured horse strikes the ground after a foot soldier takes hold of its saddle girth and its rider releases his stirrups. The dislocated bodies of the combatants and of the dead horses occupy the lower border. This scene depicts the rout of the Bretons on the left flank (scene 53).

Increasing confusion reigns in the centre of the French army. Odo - who has replaced his club with a « bâton de commandement » - stops the fleeing troops and leads them to the front (scene 54). They join Duke William who, propped on his stirrups, raises his nasal helmet and turns towards his men to show himself.

Scene 54.
Odo encouraging the Normans.

Scene 53.
The English and
the French fall
during combat.

Indeed, rumours of his death have spread. One horseman is identified as Eustace, Count of Boulogne, Edward the Confessor's brother-in-law.
The counter-attack by the Norman cavalry is supported by archers firing arrows, who are represented in the lower border (scene 55).

Scene 55. William shows himself.

The Norman horsemen are now the focus of the Tapestry. They charge, using their spears as projectiles. The English, now in a perilous situation, take shelter behind their arrow-riddled shields. A combatant from the *fyrd*, recognisable from the fact that he is wearing neither a helmet nor armour, is on the point of being decapitated (scene 56).

Scene 56. The death of Harold's companions.

The last battle scene takes place at around 5pm. Protected by his loyal followers, at the summit of a hill where he has established his command post, Harold valiantly fights against the attacking Norman archers. The arrow of an unknown archer decides on the outcome of the battle. It strikes the king's right eye. He tries to remove it before collapsing and being finished off by a horseman who thrusts a sword into his thigh. This last episode refers to the amputation of the king's body by one of Gautier Giffard's sons, who carried off the cut thigh (scene 57).

Scene 57.
Harold's standard.

Scene 57.
Harold's death.

As news of Harold's death spreads, the English soldiers group together in a gully, the Malfosse. With nightfall approaching, their desperate resistance finally weakens and they flee, pursued by the French who cause genuine carnage.

The Tapestry ends here (scene 58). It was most likely longer and a few scenes have probably disappeared... unless it was never completed. The chronicler William of Poitiers informs us that Harold's body was identified thanks to a few distinctive features and was entrusted to William Malet for burial. Duke William refused to return his remains to his mother, Gytha, who had offered its weight in gold. He may have been buried on the battlefield where, today, there is a monument in his memory in the present-day Battle Abbey (Sussex). The *Waltham Chronicle* in turn claims that Harold's body was transferred to his abbey, today the parish church of Waltham Abbey, a town in the eastern London suburbs (Essex).

Scene 58. The English flee.

A HINT OF MYSTERY...

Whose idea was it to tell the story of the Norman Conquest of England by William the Conqueror in the form of an embroidery? Who produced it? Where and when was it made? Where has it been displayed? In the absence of archives, the answers to all these questions are based on different theories. When the Tapestry was rediscovered in the early 18th century, it was defined as 'an old strip of tapestry that can now be seen in Bayeux Cathedral.' The work was never again to shake off this inadequate term of 'tapestry'.

TAPESTRY OR EMBROIDERY?

Some visitors are bewildered when they discover the Bayeux Tapestry. For the term tapestry is misleading. The work is not a decorative piece of fabric produced on a loom, its motifs being created at the same time as the fabric itself, but is an embroidery of woollen yarn applied by needle to a supporting fabric, in this case, linen.

The embroidery is made of four different stitches.

A couching stitch, referred to as 'Bayeux stitch' gives relief to the work. This stitch is produced in several stages. The first consists in tautening close pieces of yarn according to the drop stitch technique, the second in covering the first stretches of yarn perpendicularly with new yarn at 3mm intervals and, finally, in applying small stitches to fix the created design onto the canvas.

Stem stitching highlights the contours and is used to write the Latin text.

Then chain stitches and split stitches offer additional relief to certain letters and certain linear motifs.

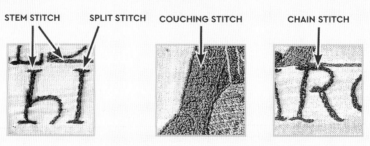

STEM STITCH   SPLIT STITCH   COUCHING STITCH   CHAIN STITCH

A second common error is the belief that the embroidery was produced by William the Conqueror's spouse, Matilda. To this very day, it is still sometimes referred to as 'Queen Matilda's Tapestry', rather than its official name of 'Bayeux Tapestry', which has the virtue of associating the town in which the work has been preserved since 1804.

Since at least the last century, historians have agreed to attribute the work's commission to Odo of Conteville.

After the conquest in which he took part, his colossal fortune was sufficient for him to effortlessly support the cost of the

Scene 43. Odo.

Tapestry's production. From his half-brother William, and in reward for his support, he received several estates along with the county of Kent, in southeast England, of which Canterbury was the most important town and with which he established important links.

St. Augustine's Abbey, Canterbury © *Fotolia*

Although many other English towns housed the embroidery workshops required to create and produce the Tapestry, it seems appropriate to favour the theory of St. Augustine's Abbey in Canterbury, renowned for its *scriptorium* and the quality of the manuscripts that were produced there. Certain illuminations may have been used as models for the Tapestry's design. Nevertheless, its production in England was recently called into question and the list of possible sponsors extended. The names of Queen Edith, Eustace of Boulogne and the Abbot Baldric of Dol have been put forward, bringing with them suggestions of other production sites including, for the latter, the Abbey of Saint-Florent of Saumur in the Loire Valley.

Inventory of the adornments of Bayeux Cathedral. Bayeux Cathedral chapterhouse library, ms 6G/199, f°95r. © AD 14 6G/199

In favour of the theory that Odo commissioned the Tapestry, is the fact that it was displayed in Bayeux Cathedral, of which he was the bishop and which he had had rebuilt. There is no evidence that it was exhibited on the 14th of July 1077, when the edifice was consecrated, even if it was most likely complete at that date. The first proof of its existence dates back to 1476, when it was described in the *Inventaire des ornements de la Cathédrale de Bayeux* as '*une tente très longue & estroicte de telle à broderie de ymages & escripteaux faisans representation du Conquest d'Angleterre, laquelle est tendue environ la nef de l'Eglise le jour & par les octaves des Reliques*' (i.e., in modern English, 'a very long and narrow hanging made of canvas embroidered with images and inscriptions representing the conquest of England, which is hung in the nave of the church by day and for eight days during the relic fair' which was held each year from the 1st to the 8th of July).

Rolled inside a chest that was part of the Treasure of Bayeux Cathedral, the Tapestry was exhibited only once yearly up to the French Revolution, encountering many serious threats throughout its existence. After being listed as a Historic Monument in 1840, thanks to Prosper Mérimée, it was offered a museographical presentation as from 1842, within the new municipal library. Listed on the Unesco 'Memory of the World' register since 2007, its greatest honour is to be among the rare French documents to be universally acknowledged and renowned.

The Bayeux Cathedral Treasure chest.
© Bayeux Museum

THE BAYEUX TAPESTRY'S KEY DATES

Late 11ᵗʰ century Creation of the Bayeux Tapestry, probably during the decade that followed 1066.

1476 First mention of the Tapestry in an inventory of the Treasure of Bayeux Cathedral.

Early 18ᵗʰ century The learned Nicolas-Joseph Foucault, intendant in Lower Normandy, discovers the Bayeux Tapestry. Antoine Lancelot and Dom Bernard de Montfaucon offer the first known representations in the form of engravings.

1792 As volunteers cover a case of weapons with the Tapestry as they leave Bayeux, Lambert Léonard Leforestier, lawyer and administrator of the district of Bayeux, replaces the Tapestry with a canvas and puts it into safe storage. Thereafter, members of the *Commission des Arts* of the district of Bayeux, watch over its fate. During the first civil fairs, they prevent it from being lacerated to adorn a float devoted to the Goddess of Reason.

1803 The Tapestry leaves Bayeux to head for Paris, where it is exhibited at the *Musée Napoléon*, later to become the Louvre. The First Consul, Napoleon Bonaparte, personally studies it. He then plans to invade England. After abandoning his plans, the Tapestry is sent back to Bayeux in 1804 to be entrusted to the inhabitants of Bayeux.

1840 The Tapestry is recorded on the first list of Historic Monuments established by Prosper Mérimée.

1842 After being stored in different sites including the Hôtel de Ville[2] in Bayeux, the Tapestry is exhibited in a glass cabinet in the municipal library's Matilda gallery.

1913 The Tapestry is moved to the Hôtel du Doyen[3], near Bayeux Cathedral.

1939–1945 The Tapestry draws many visitors among the German forces until, in the summer of 1941, Himmler sends an archaeologist, a curator specialising in fabrics, a draughtsman and a photographer on a mission to study the work. The French authorities then obtain its transfer to the Château de Sourches (Mayenne), where many other works of French heritage are stored. It leaves the store on the 26th of June 1944, officially to be taken away from the front to a safer haven in the basement of the Louvre; however, in truth, in the hope of sending it to Germany, a plan which fails thanks to the Paris insurrection. The Tapestry is exhibited in the Louvre in November and December 1944, only to return to Bayeux on the 2nd of March 1945.

1983 The Tapestry is transferred to the former great seminary in Bayeux, the vast buildings of which are more propitious than those formerly used to its correct conservation before the increasing hordes of visitors it attracts.

2007 The Bayeux Tapestry is listed on Unesco's Memory of the World Register.

2017 A project to transform the Tapestry Museum is launched by the French Prime Minister.

2. Town Hall, headquarters of the council
3. Former episcopal palace

© Jean-Yves Labartette – Bayeux Museum

Copyright general: Extracts from the Bayeux Tapestry are reproduced thanks to special authorisation from the Town of Bayeux. Unless specified otherwise, all illustrations are details of the Tapestry.

OREP Éditions, Zone tertiaire de Nonant, 14400 BAYEUX
Tel: 02 31 51 81 31 - Fax: 02 31 51 81 32
E-mail: info@orepeditions.com - Website: www.orepeditions.com
Editor: Grégory PIQUE – Graphic design: Éditions OREP
Layout: David THOUROUDE
Editorial coordination: Joëlle MEUDIC
English translation: Heather INGLIS

ISBN: 978-2-8151-0460-9
© OREP Éditions 2019
All rights reserved
Legal deposit: 1st quarter 2019